BUGATTI
CHIRON
BY EMILY ROSE OACHS

BELLWETHER MEDIA • MINNEAPOLIS, MN

Are you ready to take it to the extreme?
Torque books thrust you into the action-packed world
of sports, vehicles, mystery, and adventure. These books may
include dirt, smoke, fire, and dangerous stunts.
WARNING: read at your own risk.

This edition first published in 2018 by Bellwether Media, Inc.

No part of this publication may be reproduced in whole or in part without written permission of the publisher. For information regarding permission, write to Bellwether Media, Inc., Attention: Permissions Department, 5357 Penn Avenue South, Minneapolis, MN 55419.

Library of Congress Cataloging-in-Publication Data

Names: Oachs, Emily Rose, author.
Title: Bugatti Chiron / by Emily Rose Oachs.
Description: Minneapolis, MN : Bellwether Media, Inc., 2018. | Series:
  Torque: Car Crazy | Includes bibliographical references and index. |
  Audience: Ages 7-12.
Identifiers: LCCN 2017031293 (print) | LCCN 2017032232 (ebook) | ISBN 9781626177772
  (hardcover : alk. paper) | ISBN 9781681034829 (ebook)
Subjects: LCSH: Chiron automobile–Juvenile literature.
Classification: LCC TL215.B82 (ebook) | LCC TL215.B82 O23 2018 (print) | DDC
  629.222/2–dc23
LC record available at https://lccn.loc.gov/2017031293

Editor: Betsy Rathburn   Designer: Josh Brink

Printed in the United States of America, North Mankato, MN.

TABLE OF CONTENTS

Testing Top Speeds 4

The History of Bugatti 8

Bugatti Chiron 12

Technology and Gear 14

Today and the Future 20

Glossary 22

To Learn More 23

Index 24

TESTING TOP SPEEDS

A Bugatti Chiron slowly rounds a curve to face a long **straightaway**. Then it stops. This road has been closed to all other cars. Here, the driver can safely push the Chiron to top speeds.

The driver presses the Launch Control button on the steering wheel. Then, he steps on the gas without releasing the brake.

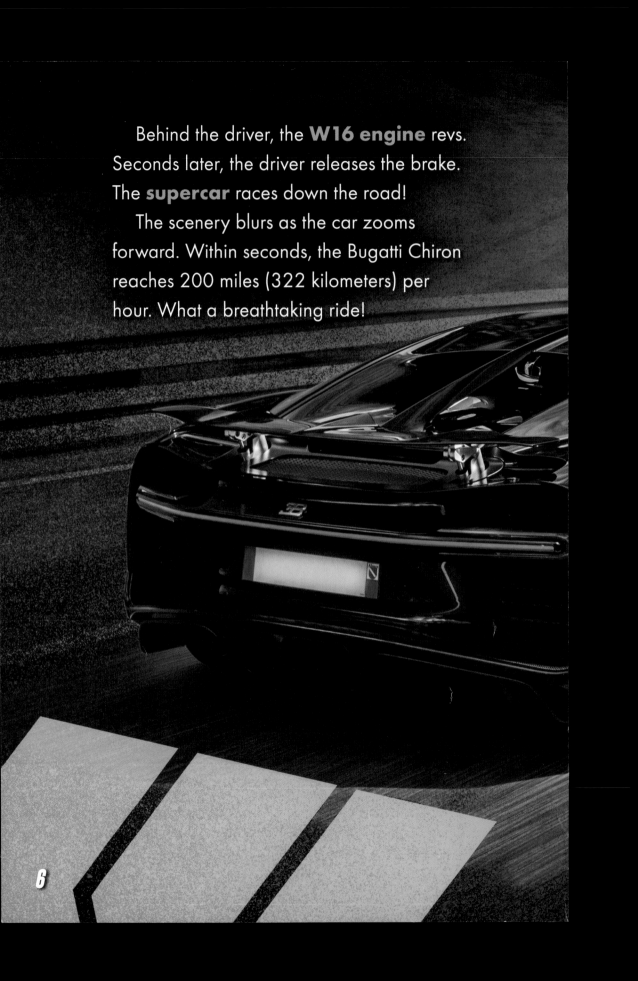

Behind the driver, the **W16 engine** revs. Seconds later, the driver releases the brake. The **supercar** races down the road!

The scenery blurs as the car zooms forward. Within seconds, the Bugatti Chiron reaches 200 miles (322 kilometers) per hour. What a breathtaking ride!

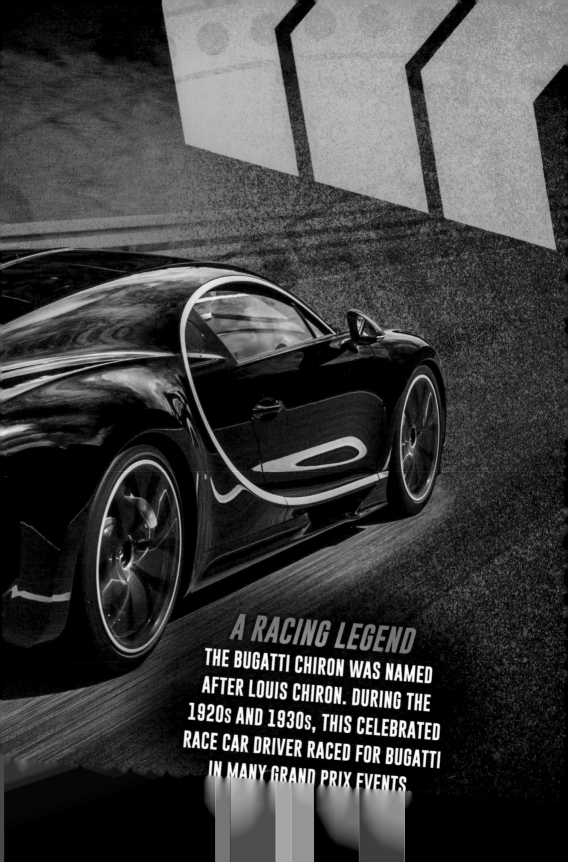

A RACING LEGEND

THE BUGATTI CHIRON WAS NAMED AFTER LOUIS CHIRON. DURING THE 1920s AND 1930s, THIS CELEBRATED RACE CAR DRIVER RACED FOR BUGATTI IN MANY GRAND PRIX EVENTS.

THE HISTORY OF BUGATTI

As a teenager, Ettore Bugatti enjoyed working on bicycles and cars. He started his own car company in 1909. Ettore's creations quickly found fame among racing fans.

Ettore Bugatti

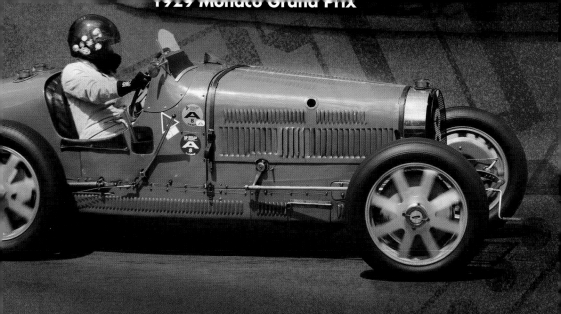

Through the 1920s and 1930s, Bugatti cars were leaders on the racetrack. They won the **24 Hours of Le Mans** and many **Grand Prix** races.

Bugatti Type 55

1999 Bugatti 18/3 Chiron

A carmaker called Volkswagen began producing Bugatti cars in 1998. Since then, the company has created some of the fastest cars in the world!

BUGATTI CHIRON

The Bugatti Chiron was introduced at the 2016 Geneva Motor Show. The new car impressed crowds with its style and power. The Chiron was soon known as one of the world's fastest **street legal** cars. It can reach speeds of 261 miles (420 kilometers) per hour!

BEYOND THE LIMITS

THE CHIRON CAN ACTUALLY TRAVEL FASTER THAN 261 MILES (420 KILOMETERS) PER HOUR. BUGATTI PLACED A LIMIT ON THE CAR'S TOP SPEED FOR SAFETY REASONS.

TECHNOLOGY AND GEAR

The Bugatti Chiron's power comes from its W16 engine. Four **turbochargers** boost the engine to 1,500 horsepower. Strong brakes help the driver stay safe.

Inside, the supercar is quiet and classy. Top-of-the-line technology makes for a comfortable driving experience. Two screens display the car's speed, **navigation**, and other information. There are even diamonds in the car's speakers!

W16 engine

HAND-SEWN SEATS

IT TAKES 16 LEATHER HIDES TO CRAFT THE INSIDE OF EACH BUGATTI CHIRON.

The Bugatti Chiron's body is made of lightweight **carbon fiber**. Its sleek shape is designed to be **aerodynamic**. Each side has a curved line that draws cooling air to the engine.

A rear **spoiler** helps the car grip the road and stop safely. It changes position at high speeds.

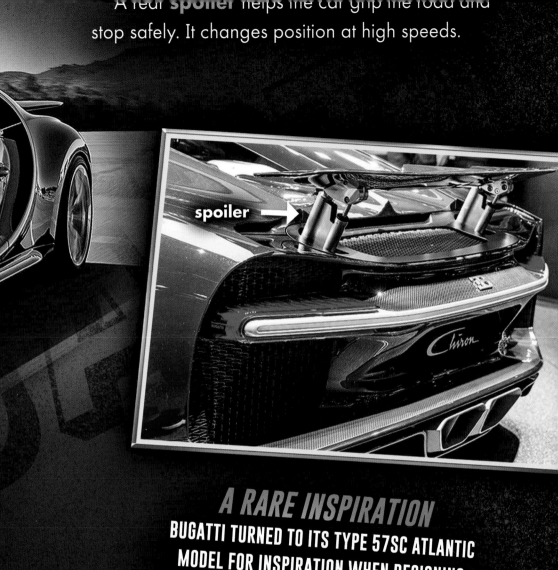

spoiler →

A RARE INSPIRATION

BUGATTI TURNED TO ITS TYPE 57SC ATLANTIC MODEL FOR INSPIRATION WHEN DESIGNING THE CHIRON. ONLY FOUR OF THOSE VEHICLES WERE EVER BUILT!

Each Bugatti Chiron has five driving modes. They adjust the car's **clearance**, steering, and **handling** to fit any situation.

A controller on the steering wheel lets drivers switch between four modes. A special key switches on the fifth mode, Top Speed. Top Speed allows drivers to push the Chiron to its limit!

2017 BUGATTI CHIRON SPECIFICATIONS

CAR STYLE	COUPE
ENGINE	8.0L W16
TOP SPEED	261 MILES (420 KILOMETERS) PER HOUR
0 - 60 TIME	ABOUT 2.4 SECONDS
HORSEPOWER	1,500 HP (1,103 KILOWATTS) @ 6,700 RPM
CURB WEIGHT	4,400 POUNDS (1,996 KILOGRAMS)
WIDTH	80.2 INCHES (204 CENTIMETERS)
LENGTH	178.9 INCHES (454 CENTIMETERS)
HEIGHT	47.7 INCHES (121 CENTIMETERS)
WHEEL SIZE	20 INCHES (51 CENTIMETERS) FRONT
	21 INCHES (53 CENTIMETERS) BACK
COST	$2.9 MILLION

TODAY AND THE FUTURE

Since its release, the Bugatti Chiron has impressed fans. People love its blend of **luxury** and speed. But the Chiron may get even better in the future.

With new technology, the Chiron may soon break its past speed records. Bugatti carries on its history of excellence with every improvement!

HOW TO SPOT A BUGATTI CHIRON

EXPOSED ENGINE   **C-SHAPED CURVES**   **REAR SPOILER**

IN SHORT SUPPLY
BUGATTI HAS ANNOUNCED THAT IT WILL PRODUCE ONLY 500 CHIRONS!

GLOSSARY

24 Hours of Le Mans—a race in which a team of drivers competes for 24 hours

aerodynamic—having a shape that can move through the air quickly

carbon fiber—a strong, lightweight material made from woven pieces of carbon

clearance—the distance between the ground and the lowest part of the car

Grand Prix—a high-level racing competition

handling—how a car performs around turns

luxury—expensive and offering great comfort

navigation—a car system that provides maps and directions to get around

spoiler—a part on the back of a car that helps the car grip the road

straightaway—the straight part of a track

street legal—able to be driven on public roads

supercar—an expensive and high-performing sports car

turbochargers—parts that increase a car's horsepower

W16 engine—an engine with 16 cylinders arranged in the shape of a "W"

TO LEARN MORE

AT THE LIBRARY

Cruz, Calvin. *Bugatti Veyron*. Minneapolis, Minn.: Bellwether Media, 2016.

Farndon, John. *Megafast Cars*. Minneapolis, Minn.: Hungry Tomato, 2016.

Goldsworthy, Steve. *Scorching Supercars*. North Mankato, Minn.: Capstone Press, 2015.

ON THE WEB

Learning more about the Bugatti Chiron is as easy as 1, 2, 3.

1. Go to www.factsurfer.com.

2. Enter "Bugatti Chiron" into the search box.

3. Click the "Surf" button and you will see a list of related web sites.

With factsurfer.com, finding more information is just a click away.

INDEX

24 Hours of Le Mans, 9

aerodynamic, 16

body, 16

brake, 5, 6, 14

Bugatti, Ettore, 8

Chiron, Louis, 7

company, 8, 10, 11, 20, 21

design, 16, 17

driving modes, 18

engine, 6, 14, 15, 16, 21

Geneva Motor Show, 12

Grand Prix, 7, 9

handling, 18

history, 7, 8, 9, 10, 11, 12, 20

how to spot, 21

interior, 14, 15

Launch Control, 5

navigation, 14

sales, 10

speakers, 14

specifications, 19

speed, 4, 6, 12, 13, 14, 17, 18, 20

spoiler, 17, 21

steering, 18

straightaway, 4

street legal, 12

supercar, 6, 14

technology, 14, 20

turbochargers, 14

Volkswagen, 11

The images in this book are reproduced through the courtesy of: P Cox/ Alamy, front cover; gyn9037, pp. 2-3; S.A.S./ Cover Images/ Newscom, pp. 4-5, 6-7, 15 (bottom); Sporti/ Wikipedia, p. 8; Peter Seyfferth/ imageBROKER/ Age Fotostock, p. 9; The Enthusiast Network/ Getty Images, p. 10; Patrick PIEL/ Getty Images, p. 11; Dong liu, pp. 12-13; DENIS BALIBOUSE/ Newscom, p. 14; Heritage Images/ Getty Images, p. 15 (top); GDA/ El Universal/ MÃ©xico/ AP Images, p. 16; Josef Horazny/ ZUMA Press, p. 17; Cover Images/ Newscom, p. 18; Maksim Toome, p. 19; Bugatti/ Cover Images/ Newscom, p. 20; Zavatskiy Aleksandr, p. 21 (top left, right); pbpgalleries/